The Return

A Play

Tony Edwards

A SAMUEL FRENCH ACTING EDITION

SAMUEL FRENCH

FOUNDED 1830

SAMUELFRENCH-LONDON.CO.UK
SAMUELFRENCH.COM

ISBN 978-0-573-12224-8

www.samuelfrench-london.co.uk

www.samuelfrench.com

FOR AMATEUR PRODUCTION ENQUIRIES

UNITED KINGDOM AND WORLD EXCLUDING NORTH AMERICA

plays@SamuelFrench-London.co.uk

020 7255 4302/01

Each title is subject to availability from Samuel French,

depending upon country of performance.

CHARACTERS

Tom Gilbert, a computer research officer
Penny Gilbert, his wife
James Scott, a computer sales manager
Alice Scott, his wife
Harry Barton, a man from Tom's past
Old Man, Harry Barton's superior

Time—the present

The action takes place in the lounge of Tom and Penny Gilbert's house

PRODUCTION NOTES

The Return is about an alien trying to hide/escape from his own kind. Since the audience are not made aware of this until the end of the play, they will wonder what is going on—which is the whole idea! Even those who suspect aliens are involved will still want to know what happens.

It is expected, however, that most will think that Tom has a crooked past and that Harry wants him to do another "job". It is important to nurture this belief, but at the same time allow "the clues" in the script to be assessed. Clues like:

"We've been to many far off places".

". . . and yes, pretended to be an ordinary human being . . ."

". . . air instead of bottled gas . . ."

"Uh, it must be child's play to you."

Penny is the overall key figure. It is her reactions of puzzlement to degrees of concern, agitated frustration to raw fear which must develop at key points so as to ensure the correct degree and build up of tension.

Question. How do you make people disappear on stage? Answer. With a simple ploy and impeccable timing! After Harry says "We should prepare", he and the Old Man move back behind the settee. During this, Tom is saying his final words to Penny. As he says "Goodbye, goodbye . . ." he is moving away from her, backwards, to join the other two men. At this point, the light and sound effects fade up, increasing as the men raise their arms. The effects get wilder with the lights flashing on and off, like lightning. It is during one of the blackout cycles, which would be fractionally longer than those preceding, that all three men simply duck down behind the settee. The effect is now enhanced by an immediate cessation of sound, simultaneous with full lights. The time between seeing the three men amid a cacophony of sound and light, to disappearance in bright, still light need be no more than two seconds.

So, build up the tension, use those effects—and please, enjoy it.

T.E.

THE RETURN *

Curtains open on to a lounge tastefully furnished, dominated by a three-piece suite embracing a coffee table. Other incidental items of furniture are neatly deployed around the room and include a drinks trolley, a small table with an exotic plant on it and an extra lounge chair.

Tom and Penny Gilbert are entertaining James and Alice Scott. The evening meal has just finished and they are repairing to the lounge for drinks. Tom works at a computer firm as research officer. He is in his late twenties/early thirties and his manner is one of quiet logic. James works at the same computer firm as sales manager. He is middle-aged, talkative, brash and, he thinks, funny. Penny is young, pretty and sensible. Alice is the same age as James. She is shrewd and tolerant. Laughter is heard off-stage just prior to them all entering the room

Penny James! You didn't really say that to him.

James Oh, yes I did, but unfortunately his sense of humour was verging on zero. It was then that I had my inspiration.

Alice Another one?

James I suddenly remembered that he was a religious nut, so I said, "Look, a computer is rather like God. Always there when needed, and when you put in the right request, you always get the right answer out!" Load of old nonsense of course, but it did the trick. He bought the whole blooming shooting match!

During the above Penny, James and Alice have sat down. Tom has gone to the drinks trolley

Penny I'm sure there was more to it than that.

James Well, perhaps just a little ...

Alice Oh, I don't know. Sounds enough to me. You and that tongue of yours could sell a false arm to an octopus.

James Funny you should mention octopus.

---

*N.B. Paragraph 3 on page ii of this Acting Edition regarding photocopying and video-recording should be carefully read.

Alice Why?
James One came limping in the other day and asked ...

Penny, Tom and Alice laugh

Penny Oh James, you are an idiot!
Alice I'll second that.

Tom has been waiting patiently by the drinks trolley

Tom If I can get a word in—what would everybody like?
Alice Drambuie, please.
Penny Same for me please, darling.
James What sort of brandy have you got, old boy?
Tom The best of course.
James I'll have a large one then.

Tom pours the drinks. Penny gets up and helps to distribute them. They then all sit

   What really sold it of course was that software package you put together, Tom. It was brilliant. How did you manage to cover all their requirements on such a small program?
Tom Do you want a technical breakdown or just a word?
Alice Since he has trouble changing a three pin plug it had better be just the word.
Tom Economy.
James Oh yes, that explains everything! Economy of what?
Tom Resources.
Alice You sound more like a good housekeeping guide than an electronic wizard.
Tom That's not a bad analogy. Making less go further or making the same do more. That's all I did.
James *All* you did! Do you know what his so called "economizing" did? It only halved the anticipated market estimate without losing any of the original applications. It wiped out any competition overnight. In fact, it's caused quite a stir. Did you know that the old man has received missives from the D.o.I. about it?
Tom Yes, he told me.
Penny The Department of Industry? Why should they be interested?
Tom They have to keep in touch with all technical developments. They need to assess the commercial benefits of new ideas.

Alice Why is that?

Tom Because new technology is accelerating at a phenomenal rate. It's bringing new industries which are changing people's lives. It affects employment, training schemes, re-deployment of labour—all of which has to be paid for.

Alice By the Government?

Tom The Government certainly contribute, if they think it's worth it. After all, it's in their own interest to see new industries develop and grow.

Penny But is this new technology so essential?

Tom One can argue essential. It's certainly inevitable.

Penny And frightening. I feel I would rather let things go their own way—a more natural progression.

James If the cavemen had thought like that we would have just finished a meal of "sabre-tooth tiger *à la spit*"...

Alice James, don't be flippant.

James ... and sitting on cold, hard rocks, which is no good at all for my ...

Alice James! Really! He's getting worse. I swear I'll have him put down. What about Penny's point Tom, about natural progression?

Tom What is natural progression? Anything that is made must, initially, come from the earth's resources. An element is found, its property discovered and exploited. Isn't that natural progression? Does natural progression preclude the use of our brains to find uses for our discoveries? Also, are not the earth's resources and our brains God given? It could be deemed an insult to Him if we were to ignore the potential of either.

James Say, aren't we beginning to get a little heavy? Earth's resources—insulting God. All I know, old chum, is that you make my job a darn sight easier. Here's to you.

Penny He's right. These computers get everywhere.

Alice I find it fascinating. Tom has a way of making the most complex of subjects sound simple, yet there's still a depth in what he says. (*She looks at James*) Makes a change from my normal level of conversation.

James Well thank you very much!

Alice How's married life treating you Penny?

James What a stupid question. You can see how it's treating her. She's radiant, blooming radiant.

Penny Flatterer.

James Laying the ground for when you get fed up with the genius.

Alice Oh, so you finally made it?

James Made what?

Alice The transition from a dirty young man to a dirty old man.

James Hey! Who are you calling old?

Penny Married life is wonderful. (*She gets up, sits on the edge of Tom's chair and kisses him*) I fully recommend it.

James Did you hear that, old girl? Perhaps we should give it a try.

Alice One day I'll disown him, so help me!

Penny All I can say is that if we're as happy together as you two are then I won't complain.

James Good Lord! You poor misguided girl. Who's been telling you those stories? I'm married to a monster. She starves me, beats me, and uses me for her own vile ends!

Alice That's just what Penny said, dear. You're happy!

Penny (*rising*) The coffee should be ready by now. Excuse me.

Penny exits

James Lovely girl you've got there.

Tom Yes, I know.

James You're a sly one! She had half the company drooling for years, then you come along and bingo! Met and married all within a couple of months. It's almost indecent!

Tom I was lucky.

James You certainly were. How many kids are you going to have?

Alice James, for goodness sake, give them a chance. They've only been married a month.

James That's more than enough time to ...

Alice James! I'm sorry Tom. He's about as sensitive as a lump of putty.

James All I was going to say was that it's never too early to think about it—plan ahead.

Alice Oh yes?

James How many in your family?

Tom Family? Just me.

James Only child, eh? Have more than one. This is a nice part of the world to bring up kids. Large town facilities with suburbs on the edge of the countryside. Perfect. All I saw as a kid was the centre of London—but Alice is a country lass, aren't you, old girl? What about you, Tom? Where were you dragged up?

Tom Um ... a small market town—up north.
James Oh? Which one?
Tom I doubt if you'll have heard of it. Newtown.
James Newtown! Another one! Do you know there's more New-towns in this country than any other name.
Alice I don't detect an accent.
Tom No. I lost it very quickly when I came south.
Alice When was that?
Tom Eh ... yes ... eh, Penny's taking a time with the coffee. I'll just check to see if everything's OK.

Tom exits

Alice I didn't know he came from up north.
James No. Actually, nobody knows much about him at all. He never talks about himself. I've heard people at work refer to him as "that strange young fellow."
Alice What did he do before joining the company?
James Haven't the foggiest. He's never said. He just appeared. Of course, everyone's glad he did. He's going to put us in number one spot.

Tom enters

Tom It apparently takes a long time to drip through the whatsit.
James Ah, that's real coffee. Well worth waiting for.
Alice We were just wondering ...

Alice is interrupted by the doorbell ringing. Mild surprise is registered because of the lateness of the hour

Alice Who on earth could that be at this hour?
James Well, let's see. It could be Mrs Thatcher come to discuss her economic policy—or a polite burglar—or ...

Penny puts her head round the door

Penny I'll get it.

Penny exits. Voices are heard in the hall. Penny re-enters

An old friend of yours, Tom. (*She stands to one side*)

Harry enters. He is an imposing figure whose presence demands immediate attention

Tom jumps to his feet

Tom My God!

There is a pause as Harry and Tom stare at each other

Harry Hello ... Tom. It's been a long time. (*He falls silent, still staring*) You do remember me, don't you Tom?
Tom Eh, yes—yes of course ...
Harry Harry. Harry Barton.
Tom Yes. What are you doing here—Harry?
Harry Just happened to be in the area and thought it would be nice to see you again—have a chat ...
Tom How did you know where I ...
Harry ... see how you're getting on.

The two men's eyes have remained locked. Penny comes between them and coughs

Tom Oh, sorry Penny. Er, Harry, this is my wife Penny ...
Penny And you are—don't tell me—Harry!
Harry Hello, Penny.
Tom And these are our friends, James and Alice Scott.

James makes to get up and shake hands but Harry makes no move towards him. James sits down again

James Good evening.
Harry Good evening.
Penny Well, eh, won't you sit down? I was just getting some coffee. Would you like some?
Harry Thank you. Black. (*He sits*)

Tom slowly sits

Penny Right. Coming up!

Penny exits

James Bit late for a visit isn't it, old man. It's nearly half past ten.
Alice James! That really is too much! I'm sorry, I'm afraid I own the world's most undiplomatic husband.
Harry (*to James*) You're quite right. It is late, but this was the only opportunity I had of seeing Tom again. It took me some time to find the address—and I've got to go back tonight.
Alice Tonight? Where to? Have you far to go?
Harry Quite a distance.

Penny enters with the coffee, distributes it and sits

James If it's not a rude question, (*glancing at Alice*) what do you
     do?
Harry I'm a traveller.
James In selling eh? That's my line. I work with Tom, you know.
     He makes 'em—I sell 'em. Computers, that is. What's your line?
Harry Import, export.
James Ah yes. I tried that once but had to give it up.
Harry Oh?
James Yes. Never knew whether I was coming or going! Ha Ha!

The only one really amused is James

     . . . ahem, eh, yes. Computers are definitely the *in* thing. Do you
     know anything about them?
Harry We do deal with certain—electronic equipment.
James Good for you. Hey, I hope it's not that foreign rubbish.
     You don't bring in that muck the Nips turn out, do you?
Harry Nips?
James No, obviously not. Good for you. Buy British. British is
     best and all that. Now if you do want a good export line you
     could do a lot worse than our little baby—or to be more
     accurate—Tom's little baby. Do you know, Tom only joined the
     company three months ago and already he's revolutionized the
     place. New designs, new programs. The blasted things can even
     diagnose their own errors and correct them! Nobody knows
     how he does it. He's a genius. A blooming genius. I could always
     call you on . . .
Alice James.
James Yes?
Alice James. Since Harry arrived to see *Tom*, they have just about
     managed to say hello to each other. Now why do you think that
     is?
James Do what?
Alice (*rising*) Come on. We're leaving these good people to a little
     peace and quiet.
Tom No, Alice, really, you don't have to go.
James (*sinking back*) Course not.
Alice Harry hasn't seen Tom for—how long, Harry?
Harry Three years.

Alice Three years—and they've only got a short while now for a chat, so don't argue. Go! (*She pulls James up and pushes him towards the door*) Nice to meet you, Harry. Thank you for a lovely dinner, Penny. (*She kisses Penny*) Thank you, Tom. (*She kisses Tom*) Don't forget. It's our turn next Wednesday.

Penny exits then returns with Alice's and James' coats. She escorts them to the door with many goodbyes; then returns and sits once more on the arm of Tom's chair

Penny Whew! (*She sips her coffee*) Poor old Alice. James is a lovely man, but can be so wearing!

The men do not comment. Penny takes another sip of coffee

Penny Well, Harry. How long have you known Tom?
Harry Quite a few years.
Penny Where did you meet?
Tom (*quickly*) I used to work with Harry.
Harry We used to travel around together. They were good days.
Penny You mean abroad?
Harry Oh yes. We've been to many far off places. (*He looks from Tom to Penny*) Hasn't Tom told you about them?
Penny No, he hasn't mentioned it. You see, we've only been married a month. It was your classical whirlwind romance. Thinking about it, we don't really know a lot about each other, do we Tom?
Tom No, not really. As you say, things happened so quickly.
Penny (*hugging him*) But I don't mind. We've got the rest of our lives to find out. Anyway, that's one of the things I like about Tom. Quiet, enigmatic even. He makes me feel—safe. Although sometimes he frightens me.
Tom (*concerned*) Frighten? I frighten you? How?
Penny 'Cause you're so blooming clever! A blooming genius as James would say.
Tom I don't want to frighten you. I never meant to.
Penny (*laughing*) Don't look so serious, darling. I don't mean "scared" frightened. It's just that sometimes, I wonder, wonder if I can keep up with you—your brain—your intellect. I don't want to be a bore for you—or ... (*She realizes she is going too deep*) ... oh, I'm being silly—in front of Harry.
Harry (*to Tom*) I wanted to talk to you about the business.

Tom The business? What about it?
Harry It's still going strong.
Tom Good.
Harry Although not as strong as it could be.
Tom What are you saying?
Harry We want you back.
Tom That's nice of you to say so, but that's impossible.
Harry Impossible?

Tom gets up and pours himself another drink. He remains standing

Tom My work, my home. Everything's different now. I couldn't possibly afford the time. You can't need me. Not after all this time.
Harry But we do. We were never able to replace you.
Tom I'm settled here now. Married, a good job. I can't just walk away from them.
Harry It's never been the same since you left. No one else was able to do your job as well as you did it.
Tom That's as may be, but I've got other commitments, other responsibilities now. When I left it was a clean break. No turning back. I made that decision then and I see no reason to change it.
Harry You know how important our work is. We know you had your reasons. There is—higher reward—in this ...
Tom Higher reward! So, you finally got round to realising ...
Harry ... and all that goes with it.
Tom (*deliberately*) No.
Harry Have you thought ...?
Penny (*interrupting*) Excuse me Harry, but if I'm getting the drift of this, you're offering Tom his old job back? Import, export?
Harry Yes.
Penny Does that include going abroad?
Harry Away, yes.
Penny Um. Well, for my part—and I am involved after all, I agree with Tom. I certainly don't fancy uprooting so soon after moving in. As for not seeing him for days, possibly weeks at a time—no thank you! (*She holds Tom's hand*)
Tom So, thanks for the offer, Harry, but you see how it is.
Harry Things have changed a lot. The old problems—shouldn't happen again. You would be much happier with the new arrangements.

Tom New arrangements? Higher rewards? They've come a bit late haven't they? In fact, much too late.

Harry You left at a critical time. There were still things to be done—important things.

Tom Surely you've dealt with them by now? Are you telling me the business is unsuccessful?

Harry Let's say it's ticking over. We're certainly not making the progress we want to—mainly because we've lost your—special skills.

Tom But it's been three years . . .

Harry Which only emphasizes the point—the size of the problem.

Penny Look Harry. As I see it, you've got this problem with your business which Tom could—help out—with, so you're offering him his old job back. That's fine. But the point you seem to be missing is that we have only just settled in here. You see, we were only married a month ago and you heard James say what an impact Tom has made with the company after only three months. Things are—well, they're just perfect here. We would be silly—irresponsible even, if we changed things now. Surely you can see that!

Harry turns his head slowly towards Penny and smiles thinly

Harry Yes. (*Pause*) Is there any more coffee?

Penny is taken slightly unawares

Penny Of course. (*She goes to the coffee pot*)
Harry Fresh coffee?

Penny stops

Penny Yes, of course. It'll take a few minutes.

   Penny exits with the tray, an uncertain look on her face

Tom watches Penny go, then strides over to Harry

Tom How the hell did you find me?
Harry We have our methods—you should know that . . . Tom.
Tom In that case, why wait three years? Why let me think I'd got rid of you—all of you?
Harry For a while it was thought possible that we could do without you, but it was no good. You are too much of a specialist.

Tom (*slowly*) I'm not coming back. Say what you like. I'm not coming back.

Harry What about the others?

Tom What about them?

Harry It affects all of them. All hand picked. Years of training. Working together as a team. Then suddenly you decide to opt out. Where does it leave them? The projects?

Tom Don't give me that! Don't try to say you didn't know what was going on. They brought it on themselves. Jealousies and lies. Undermining my authority. Questioning my decisions. Each job became more dangerous—I couldn't rely on anybody. Somebody would have ended up getting killed. I warned you often enough, but you chose to ignore it. Oh no, don't ask me to think of them now. I'm out, and I'm staying out!

Harry I told you. Things have changed. New arrangements. You won't have that trouble again. Even so, your actions were somewhat drastic—just walking out. You had no right to do that—and then to hide, knowing what you know.

Tom That's it, isn't it? It's what I know. You don't care about me.

Harry The one goes with the other.

Tom You don't have to worry. No one knows about me—and they never will as long as I'm left in peace.

Harry (*Going to Tom*) You've got to come back.

Tom No! And you can't make me.

The faces are close. Pause, and Harry breaks away

Harry Look, there's something big happening soon, you know the sort of thing, and we've got to be ready for it. Without you, we won't be.

Tom That's your problem, not mine.

For the first time Harry approaches anger, but he is still controlled

Harry Wrong! It's yours as well. Do you really think you can just leave? Walk away—take up another life? Get a job, get married like everyone else, as if your past—us—never existed? You think you can become an ordinary person? Think you can belong here? No! Nothing will ever change who you really are. You can pretend all you like, but it's there, deep down inside, the real you. You might want to, but you can't deny it.

Tom I can try! What you don't realise is that it's not just the others—you—the business. When I came here and, yes, pretended to be an ordinary human being, I found I wanted it for what it was. It's got a simple beauty. For the first time I really feel part of something. Here, I look up and see a sun, not neon light. There are trees instead of metal, grass instead of plastic, air instead of bottled gas. Don't tell me I don't belong here. It's the only place I do belong. Yes, I am who I am, but I can adapt. I'm not going back.

Harry (*now composed*) And your wife knows nothing about you, your previous work?

Tom And she won't!

Harry I could so easily tell her.

Tom But you won't!

Harry I wouldn't be so absolutely sure about that if I were you.

Tom I said ...

Harry Though I don't suppose that will be necessary, since I'm sure you'll see that it's best to come back of your own accord.

Tom How many times must I tell ...?

Harry Made any mistakes yet?

Tom What?

Harry Mistakes. Anything slipped out in an unguarded moment? The odd word or phrase that doesn't quite fit in with your ... new life. Something that will raise the dreaded question, "What do you mean, Tom?" Something that will trigger the curious mind so that it insists on an explanation—and you can't give it. Oh yes, you can lie, but for how long? How often! All your life? A life that doesn't belong here.

Tom Yes, yes, I know. I've thought of all that. I know there's a risk, and I'm prepared to take it; even though it might mean ... avoiding the truth sometimes. But Penny is special. She wouldn't push a point. She wouldn't force the issue, she ...

Harry But it's not just Penny, is it? There's your friends, people at work. They'll all want to know more about you as time goes on. Especially since you seem to be doing rather well—a blooming genius. Uh, it must be child's play to you.

Penny enters with the coffee

Penny Sorry it's taken so long. (*She pours each a cup*) I heard you mention children, Harry. Have you got any?

Harry Yes, four.

Penny Lovely! What mix?
Harry Three male, one female.

Penny frowns slightly at this description

Penny Are they still at school or working?
Harry They are all still—learning. Do you like children?
Penny Oh yes, very much.
Harry So you plan to have a family?
Penny We have touched on the subject, haven't we, Tom? We think, that is, Tom thinks we should wait and see how things are after a couple of years.
Harry But you don't agree?
Penny Well yes, I do to a point. As Tom so quaintly puts it, "You shouldn't lay eggs before the nest is built", but I think two years is rather a long time.
Harry Yes. (*He looks at Tom*) The females always seem to have a more pressing desire for children, don't they?
Tom Yes, I suppose they do.
Harry How many children do you want?
Tom Er, I don't really know. As Penny says, we've hardly discussed it.
Harry All I can say is that if they inherit your obvious brains and Penny's good looks they'll really be something special.
Penny Every child is special to someone.

Pause, Tom looks at his watch and rises

Tom Well, Harry, it was great to see you again. Thanks very much for the offer. I'm sure you'll be wanting to ...
Harry I can't leave without you.

They all freeze. Penny looks at Tom, puzzled

Penny I ... I thought all that was settled?
Tom It is!
Harry No, I'm afraid it's not. Our next project is big, very big. There is much at stake. Nothing must go wrong. It's essential, vital that we have you with us.
Penny One project? How long would it last? Tom—if it's as important as Harry says, and you weren't away too long, perhaps you could help ...
Tom No. It's not as easy as that. If I went there would be other

jobs—other projects to which I would be vital, wouldn't there, Harry?

Harry That's for not for me to say. All I know is you're needed now.

Penny If it was made clear that it was just the once, Tom—from whoever is in charge. It does sound terribly important. What exactly is . . .

Tom (*sharply*) Penny, for God's sake keep out of it. You don't understand.

Penny is aghast at Tom's tone

Penny Tom! I was only trying to compromise. To say I wouldn't mind a temporary absence. Why not?

Harry "Trigger the curious mind".

Penny What does that mean?

Harry "The dreaded question".

Penny (*getting agitated*) Tom, tell me. What does he mean?

Harry "Insisting on an explanation".

Tom Penny, just leave it. We'll talk later—when Harry's gone.

Penny looks from one to the other, then decides. She stands in front of Harry

Penny Goodnight Harry.

Harry doesn't move

Penny Harry. It's late. Goodnight!

Harry just stares at Penny

Penny O K, Harry—that's enough. Something is obviously going on here. I don't know what. What I do know Tom is staying and you are leaving—one way or the other.

Harry Now I insist.

Penny (*exploding*) Like hell you do!

Tom Penny, keep out of it!

Penny What does he mean, insist? Coming here, telling you what to do. *Who is he?*

Harry Aaah! Who am I, Tom?

Tom (*going to Harry*) Someone who's leaving now.

Harry You're coming back.

Tom (*grabbing Harry*) No! Never again! You've misjudged me this time. I got out, and nothing and no one will get me to return. You can't insist. (*He is shaking Harry*) You haven't got the authority, or the power—and you know it.

Penny grabs Tom and pulls him away

Penny Tom! Stop it! Stop it! (*She turns on Harry*) And you, get out!

Harry ignores Penny

Harry No. I haven't got the power—but there is someone who has.
Penny Get out! Now!
Tom No one is going to make me . . .

Tom's voice trails away. A long pause as realization dawns on his face. His jaw drops. He stares at Harry, who is nodding slowly

Harry Yes, him.
Tom (*dazed*) You . . . you're bluffing. He wouldn't come here, he couldn't . . . he . . .
Harry I told you it was that important—vital.
Penny Tom! What is he . . . who is he talking about?
Tom No! No, I don't believe you. He can't be here.
Penny Tom, for God's sake tell me what is . . .?

The doorbell rings. The three freeze. A look of sheer terror slowly comes to Tom's face

Penny, fearful, goes to answer the door

Tom sinks into a chair moaning

Tom No! Please, no!

Penny enters, followed by an elderly man. She is angrily quizzing him

Penny . . . and I want to know why my husband is being put under this pressure to do something he doesn't want to do—and then you and this . . . gentleman can leave. Otherwise I'll call . . .

The Old Man has not been listening from the start. He has been staring at Tom, who has been staring back in disbelief

Old Man Hello Tom. We've missed you.

Tom No, please! Don't make me, please.

Penny (*shocked*) Tom!

Old Man You know you can't just leave like that. It breaks the rules. The rules are made for your safety, our safety, everyone's safety. You know that. Deep down, you know that.

Tom Just one. It won't make any difference. Just one. Just me.

Old Man One is the same as a hundred and one.

Penny Tom, for pity's sake. What is he doing to you?

Harry We should prepare.

Harry and the Old Man move behind the settee

Penny Tom?

Tom turns to Penny. He holds her hands. His face is haggard, beaten

Tom Penny, my love ... I'm sorry. I tried to hide from them. I thought I had. I never thought they would find me. Not after three years. This planet was the most beautiful of all. Your life form the perfect escape—to start again. To be an individual and not a ... I can't stop them. Not both of them. They have the power ... the power ... I'm sorry my love. Goodbye ... goodbye ... goodbye ...

Tom has backed away to join the other men. While he has been speaking strange lights and sounds have filled the room. The men are looking up, their arms raised as if in offering. A beam of light falls on them. The sounds and lights swirl. The three aliens disappear. The swirling lights and sounds cease. Penny has been frozen to the spot in open-mouthed horror. Now she stumbles to where the three men were, desperately looking around and up. Then her fears explode into one long scream. At its height, the scream is cut off simultaneously with total Black-out*

The CURTAIN *falls*

*See Production Note.

FURNITURE AND PROPERTY LIST

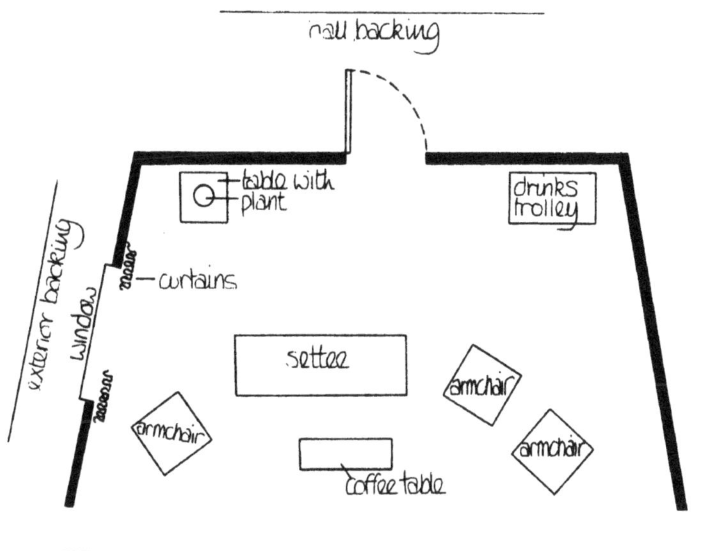

On stage: Three-piece suite
Lounge chair
Coffee table
Drinks trolley. *On it:* glasses,
various bottles, including Drambuie and
brandy bottles
Small table. *On it:* exotic plant
Other furniture at Director's discretion

Off stage: Tray. *On it:* coffee pot, five cups
milk jug and sugar bowl **(Penny)**
Two coats **(Penny)**
Coffee pot, refilled **(Penny)**

LIGHTING PLOT

To open: General interior lighting

Cue 1*   **Tom:** "Penny, my love . . . I'm sorry."   (Page 16)
Gradually fade up "weird" lighting

Cue 2*   The three men raise their arms   (Page 16)
Beam of light on the three men;
lights swirl and flash.
Once actors have disappeared in short
blackout
Lights back to normal

Cue 3   Penny's scream stops   (Page 16)
Blackout

*See Production Note

EFFECTS PLOT

Cue 1 **Alice:** "We were just wondering ..." (Page 5)
   Doorbell rings

Cue 2 **Penny:** "Tom, for God's sake tell me
   what is ..." (Page 15)
   Doorbell rings

Cue 3* **Tom:** "Penny, my love ... I'm sorry" (Page 16)
   Gradually fade up "weird" sounds

Cue 4* The three men raise their arms (Page 16)
   Weird sounds increase; once actors
   have disappeared, *cut sounds*

*See Production Note

9 780573 122248